The Donner Party Cookbook

1847: The Donner Party is rescued after being snowbound in the Sierra Nevadas. Almost half of the group died, and some of the original settlers seemed to be oddly well-fed, considering the ordeal they went through. Cannibalism is no crime, however, and charges were never brought.

Donner Party Cookbook

Casseroles, Just Desserts, and Helpful Advice for Travelers

Published by
THREE DOG PUBLISHING
3250 Kingsley Drive, Florissant, Mo. 63033

Copyright 2014

No parts of this book may be reprinted without permission unless we say so, or unless you have lots of "lettuce" or "cabbage."

Created by
Paul and Nancy Marasa

The Donner Party Cookbook

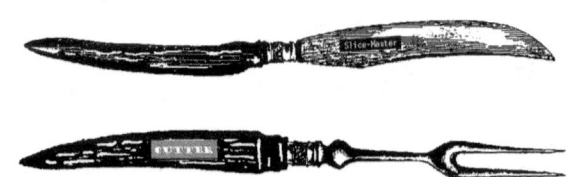

can'nibal one who eats human flesh.
can'ni'bal'ism *noun* \be-,liz-em
  1: the usually ritualistic eating of human flesh by a human being *(but not in their case)*.

The Donner Party Cookbook

👉 INDEX OF RECIPES 👈

Maude's Beef Tingler 2
Stormy Day Bean Soup 4
Old Settler's Beans 6
Cabbage & Noodles Conestoga 6
Sierra Nevada Potatoes 8
Shepherd's Pie 10
Blizzard Pie 10
Wiener Schnitzel -Donner 12
Pawnee Pigeon Pie 14
Family Goulash 16
Old-Fashioned Oxtail Stew 18
Steak Diane (or whoever) 20
Cousin Zeb's Wieners 22
Party Wieners 22
German Braised Kidneys 24
Tongue with Horseradish Sauce 26
"Forlorn Hope" Meat Platter Deluxe 28
Quick Company Steak in Foil 30
Salt Lake Mutton Bake 30
Gertrude Donner's Beef Pockets 32
Crepe Suzette 34
Tamzene's White Mountain Cake 36
Snowy Apple Salad 38
Sutter's Fort Sorbet 38
Calves Foot Jelly 40
Applesauce Relish 40

No humans were cannibalized in the making of the book...at least, not yet!

IV

The Donner Party Cookbook

Notes

Maude's Beef Tingler
(Much tastier than Cream of Yesterday).

2 10-1/2 cans condensed beef broth
2 soup cans water
1/4 cup Frangelico
1/4 cup heavy cream
1/8 tsp. vanilla
dash of ginger
1/8 tsp. grated orange rind

In a saucepan, combine soup, water and brandy. Heat, stirring occasionally. Meanwhile, in a small bowl, combine cream, vanilla and nutmeg. Beat until cream just mounds. Fold in orange rind. *Serve on soup.* (What is dis schlop, anyway?)
Servings: 5 1/2 cups.

Soup Quantities For Large Parties
25 servings: 1-1/2 Gallons
50 servings: 3 Gallons
100 servings: Never Mind...

Overheard on the trail:
"Will you join me in a bowl of soup? It's big enough for both of us."

Thanks for the buggy ride...

"The Pioneer Palace Car" *was the flagship of the Donner Party. It was a luxurious 2-story affair with a built-in stove, padded seats, and bunks for sleeping. The wagon deluxe was pulled by a team of eight oxen. (The owner's manual included a bus schedule and directions for braking while rolling downhill).*

Overheard on the trail:
"What is a wagon with a moonroof? A land yacht."

Stormy Day Bean Soup

(So thick that when you stir it, the room goes round).

1 pound dried navy beans
7 cups water
1 ham bone
2 cups cubed cooked smoked ham
1/4 cup minced onion
1/2 tsp. salt
1 bay leaf
Dash pepper

   Rinse beans. Heat beans and water to boiling; boil gently 2 minutes. Remove from heat; cover and let stand 1 hour.
   Add remaining ingredients. Heat to boiling. Reduce heat; cover and simmer about 1 hour and 15 minutes or until beans are soft. Skim off foam occasionally (add water if necessary).
   Remove bay leaf and ham bone. Trim meat from bone; add to soup. Season to taste.
7 Servings.

Overheard on the trail:
"I love people, smothered in gravy."
"How do you make gold soup?" "With 22 carrots."

Notes

Culinary Hint for the Ladies:
"Butterflies in his stomach will make a lovely garnish".

Old Settler's Beans
(Generates plenty of gas to warm up the camp).

4 slices bacon, cut up
1 large onion chopped
1/2 green pepper diced
1 lb. hamburger

Cook til just turns color in a skillet. Pour off excess grease.

1 cup brown sugar
1 cup catsup
1 can pork & beans (1 lb., 5 oz.)
1 can red beans (drained)
1 small can lima beans

Add to above. Bake for 45 minutes covered, then remove lid and bake 15 minutes more at 325.

Cabbage And Noodles Conestoga
(Cabbage always has a heart).

1 large head cabbage, chopped
1 stick margarine
1 (12 oz.) pkg. egg noodles
1 medium onion

Fry cabbage in margarine. Add onion. Cook noodles as directed on package. When cabbage and onion mixture is tender, add the cooked and drained noodles. Mix well and serve.

4 servings.

Overheard on the trail:
"I'm going to miss me when I'm gone."

The Donner Party Cookbook

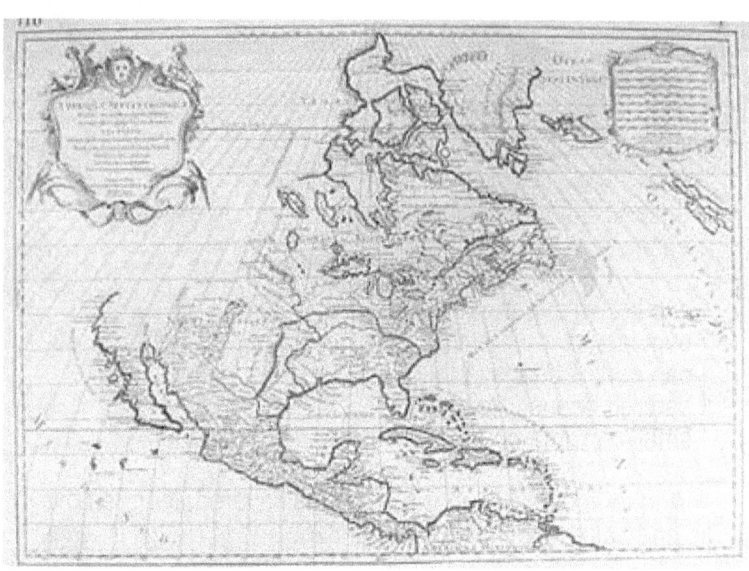

 ## *"Where the heck is California?"*

We wuz lookin' to settle in a different state,
but Californy seemed to levitate.
We looked high and peered down low.
Where that state wuz, we didn't know.
Sure could've used a GPS,
but lacking that, we headed west (?).

Advice from the trail:
"When everything else fails, read the map.."

Sierra Nevada Potatoes

(If you hate your mother-in-law, try the potatoes).

For each serving:
1 baking potato
1 1/2 teaspoons evaporated milk
1 teaspoon butter
salt
sweet paprika

   Pierce the well-scrubbed potato with the tip of the knife. Bake at 350 degrees until done, about 1 hour. The potato will feel soft when it's squeezed (***ouch***).
   Cut a wide cross in the potato, and spread the peel back a little. Insert a fork into the opening and mash the tater slightly. Pour in the milk, and poke the butter well into the potato. Sprinkle with a bit of salt and a dash of paprika.

Advice from the trail:
"You can duplicate the warmth of a down-filled
bedroll by climbing into a plastic garbage bag with several geese."

The Donner Party Cookbook

Notes

Shepherd's Pie *A.K.A. Blizzard Pie

(An old favorite on the trail).

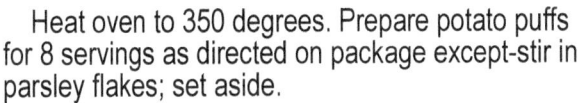

Instant mashed potato puffs
2 tablespoons parsley flakes
2 cups cubed cooked lamb, beef or veal
1/4 cup chopped onion
2 cups cooked vegetables (peas, carrots or corn)
2 cups gravy*

Heat oven to 350 degrees. Prepare potato puffs for 8 servings as directed on package except-stir in parsley flakes; set aside.

In ungreased 3-quart casserole, stir together remaining ingredients. Mound potatoes on meat mixture. Bake uncovered 30 minutes or until potatoes brown slightly.

6 Servings.

*2 cans (10 3/4 ounces each) gravy can be used.

The Donner Party left Missouri on May 12, 1846. There were 9 wagons, 31 people and 2 rolls of duct tape. Destination: Sutter's Fort, California. *Wagons ho!*

The Donner Party Cookbook

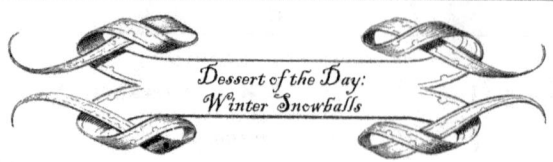

Dessert of the Day: Winter Snowballs

Get romantic for dinner...nibble on her ear...

"Poetry from the Trail"

With the wagons pointed West,
they gave it their best.
The snow began falling,
the kids started bawling,
and we know the inevitable rest...

Wiener Schnitzel-Donner
(For hearty appetites).

4 veal cutlets (about 4 ounces each)
   or 1-pound veal round steak, 1/2 inch thick
1/2 cup all-purpose flour*
1 teaspoon salt
1/2 teaspoon paprika
1/4 teaspoon pepper
1 egg
2 tablespoons water
1 cup dry bread crumbs
1/4 cup shortening
1 lemon, cut into wedges

   If using veal round steak, cut into 4 pieces. Mix flour, salt, paprika and pepper. Coat meat with flour mixture; pound until 1/4 inch thick. Beat egg and water until blended. Dip meat into egg mixture, then coat with bread crumbs.

   Melt shortening in large skillet; brown meat quickly. Reduce heat; cover and cook about 45 minutes or until tender. Serve with lemon wedges.

4 Servings.

Overheard on the trail:
"I like cats, too. Let's exchange recipes."
"If you're not the lead oxen, the scenery never changes."

The Donner Party Cookbook

Notes

Pawnee Pigeon Pie
(This will make your heart flutter & melt your butter).

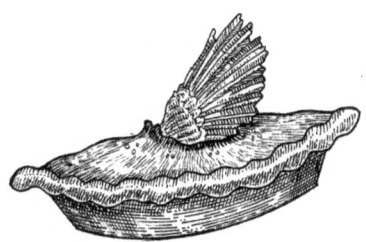

4-5 pigeons, drawn
salt and pepper
8 oz. stewing beef
8 oz. piecrust pastry
beaten egg to glaze
2 tsp. cornflour
10 oz. stock

Preheat oven to 350 F. Joint the birds into 2 breast and 2 leg joints and stew the rest in water to make gravy stock. Cut beef into small pieces and line a deep 8" pie dish with these. Lay the pigeon joints on top, cover with water, add salt and pepper, then cover pie dish with aluminum foil. Place in oven & simmer for 1-1/2 hours.

Remove from oven & raise temp to 400 F. Cover pie with pastry, brush the top with beaten egg, put back in oven & bake until golden brown.

Make gravy by stirring cornflour with a little cold water and add to 10 oz. of stock. Allow to thicken while stirring, season and stir.

6 Servings.

A Donner Party Limerick:
*"On the trail to Sutter
she ceased to mutter
when good ol' Doc
chopped her up in a crock,
and seasoned with onion & butter."*

For a change of pace, sprinkle with dry bread crumbs.

"Poetry from the Trail"

There once was a Donner named Tamsen,
who was held a short time for ransom:
*"Give us your liver,
and don't even quiver,
and throw in your big friend, Samson."*

Family Goulash

(This is the perfect opportunity to sink your teeth into that big family in the next cabin. Enjoy!)

4 ounces fine noodles
1 pound ground beef (or liver)
1 medium onion, chopped (about 1/2 cup)
2 cups sliced celery
1/2 cup catsup
1 jar (2 1/2 ounces) sliced mushrooms
1 can (14 1/2 ounces) tomatoes
2 teaspoons salt
1/4 teaspoon pepper

Cook noodles as directed by pouring into large, salted pot of boiling water. Cook for 10 minutes. While noodles cook, stir and saute ground beef and onion in large skillet until meat is brown and onion is tender. Drain off fat.

Stir in drained noodles, celery, catsup, mushrooms (with liquid), tomatoes, salt, and pepper. Cover; simmer 30 to 45 minutes.

4 Servings.

Advice from the campfire:
"If you're given the cold shoulder, wash it down with beer."
"Butter up your neighbor, and serve him with a smile."

Notes

Old-Fashioned Oxtail Stew

(Yokes aside-this is worth the effort).

1/2 cup all-purpose flour
1 teaspoon salt
1/4 teaspoon pepper
4 pounds oxtails, cut into 1-inch pieces
2 tbsp. shortening
6 cups hot water
3 pared medium potatoes, cut into 1-inch cubes
1 medium turnip, cut into 1-inch cubes
4 carrots, cut into 1-inch pieces
1 green pepper, cut into strips
1 cup sliced celery
1 medium onion, diced
1 tbsp. salt
2 beef bouillon cubes
1 bay leaf

   Mix flour, 1 teaspoon salt and the pepper. Coat meat with flour mixture. Melt shortening in large skillet; brown meat thoroughly.

   Add water; heat to boiling. Reduce heat; cover and simmer 3 and 1/2 hours. Stir in remaining ingredients. Simmer 30 minutes or until veggies are tender.

   If desired, thicken stew. In covered small jar, shake 1 cup cold water and 2 to 4 tbsp. flour until blended. Stir into stew; heat to boiling, stirring constantly. Boil and stir 1 minute.

6 Servings.

General rule of your neighbor's thumb:
Most food cannot be kept for longer than the average human lifespan

The Donner Party Cookbook

Notes

Steak Diane (Or Jacob or...)
(Where's the beef?).

1/2 cup thinly sliced fresh mushrooms
2 tablespoons minced onion
1 clove garlic
1/8 tsp. salt
1 tsp. lemon juice
1 tsp. worcestershire sauce
1/4 cup butter or margarine
1 tablespoon snipped parsley
2 tablespoons butter or margarine
1-pound beef tenderloin, cut into 8 slices

Cook and stir mushrooms, onion, garlic, salt, lemon juice and Worcestershire sauce in 1/4 cup butter until mushrooms are tender. Stir in parsley; keep sauce warm.

Melt 2 tablespoons butter in skillet; turning once, cook tenderloin slices over medium-high heat to medium doneness, about 3 to 4 minutes on each side. Serve with mushroom-butter sauce.

4 Servings.

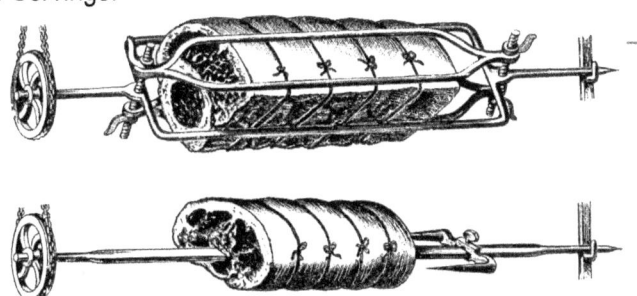

Philosophy from the trail:
"A balanced diet is a humerus in each hand."
"The journey of a thousand miles begins with a broken wagon wheel and stubborn oxen."

The Donner Party Cookbook

Dateline: 1846

Tamsen Donner, wife of George Donner, sent this message from Independence to her sister Eliza Poor: *"It is supposed there be 7000 waggons start from this place, this season. We go to California."* (Modern research puts the actual number of wagons at about 250, with approximately 1500 people, headed for both California and Oregon).

"But I followed the recipe. What went wrong? Could it have been my clever **substitutions**?"

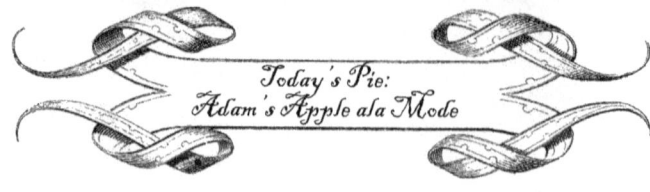

Today's Pie: Adam's Apple a la Mode

The Donner Party Cookbook

Cousin Zeb's Wieners
(There he goes, showing off his wiener again.)

8 slices bacon, diced
3 cups minced onion
1 can (16 ounces) tomatoes
1/2 cup catsup
1/4 teaspoon salt
1/8 teaspoon pepper
1 pound frankfurters

In large skillet, fry bacon and onion until bacon is crisp and onion is tender. Drain all but 2 tablespoons bacon drippings from skillet. Stir in tomatoes, salt and pepper. Heat to boiling; reduce heat and simmer 15 minutes, stirring occasionally. Add frankfurters, cover and simmer 15 minutes.

5 or 6 Servings.

 ### Party Wieners

Frankfurters, Vienna sausages or cocktail wieners
1/3 cup prepared mustard
1/2 cup grape jelly

Cut meat in bite-size pieces. Mix mustard and jelly in 1-quart saucepan. Add meat. Cover and cook at low heat for 10 minutes. Serve on toothpicks with crackers. Makes 3/4 cup sauce.

Notes

German Braised Kidneys
(Donors welcomed-no rejections).

6 veal kidneys
2 cups water
2 tablespoons vinegar
4 tablespoons butter
1 cup chopped onion
1-1/2 teaspoon salt
1/4 teaspoon pepper
2 tablespoons minced parsley
1/2 cup sour cream

   Wash the kidneys, cut in half and discard the cores. Soak in the water mixed with vinegar 1 hour. Drain and slice very thin. Melt the butter in a skillet; saute the onions 5 minutes. Add the kidneys and cook until browned. Mix in the salt, pepper, sour cream; cook over low heat 5 minutes. Sprinkle with parsley.

5 or 6 Servings.

Advice from the trail:
"When smoking a fish, do not inhale."
"You'll never be lost if you remember that moss always grows on the north side of your compass."

"Dinner of Last Resort"

1 helping of **rough terrain**,
Season with **many delays**,
Cover with a **heavy snowfall**.

*This is a recipe for disaster and serves *45.*

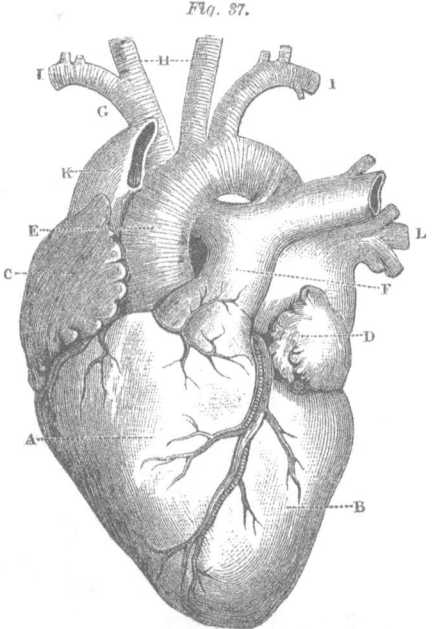

*There were 45 survivors of the Donner Party.

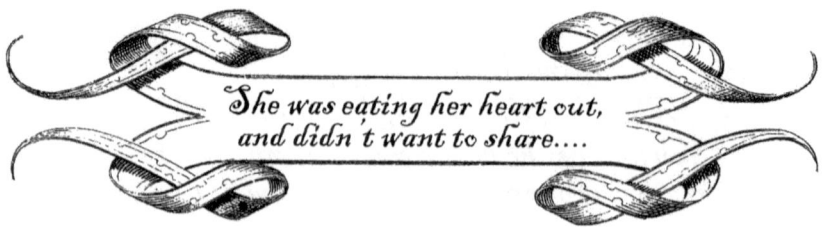

She was eating her heart out, and didn't want to share....

Tongue (in cheek) with Horseradish Sauce

(Tickle your taste buds with this delicacy).

5 lb. smoked or pickled beef tongue
1/2 cup prepared horseradish
1/3 cup soft bread crumbs
1 cup sour cream
2 tablespoons butter
1 egg yolk
lt. prepared mustard

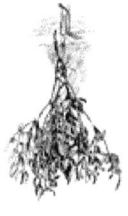

Wash tongue, cover with water, and bring to boil. Cover and cook over low heat 3 hours, or until tongue is tender. As the water boils out, add boiling water so tongue is covered at all times. Drain, reserving 1 cup of liquid. Remove the root ends, bones, and skin of the tongue. *You don't really want to know more, do you?*

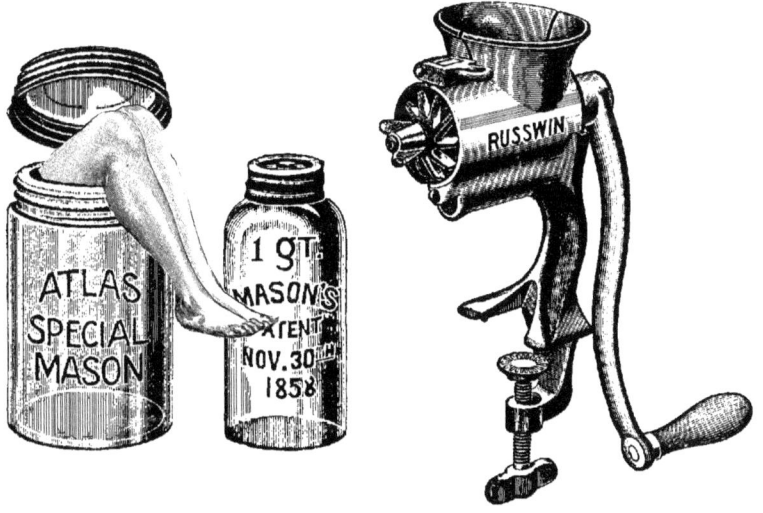

"The tongue weighs practically nothing, but so few people can hold it."

Notes

Advice to the Carver:
"Don't try to cheat me! I see your finger on the scale."

"Forlorn Hope" Meat Platter Deluxe

(Putting a foot in your mouth never tasted so good.)

1/4 pound liver sausage, cut into 1/4-inch slices
6 slices cooked salami (about 3 ounces)
6 slices large bologna (about 3 ounces)
6 slices pickle and olive loaf (about 4 ounces)
6 slices Swiss cheese (about 5 ounces)
6 wedges Edam cheese (about 6 ounces)
green onions, washed and trimmed
pimiento-stuffed small olives
1 medium cucumber, washed, scored with fork
  and cut into 1/4 inch slices
sweet pickles
spiced crab apples

Arrange ingredients on large serving plate.

6 servings.

"There were tracks in the snow, leading right to the door. Now them folks ain't been seen no more."

The Donner Party Cookbook

"Good Bread Will Have a Nutty Flavor and a Pale Creamy Tint."

General Housekeeping in 1846:
This lovely lady would have had a book of domestic receipts (recipes). The most formidable labor for the young and inexperienced woman was that of making bread. The best dough was spent paying the local baker to supply the family's needs.

Quick Company Steak in Foil

("How to serve your fellow man").

5 cubed, minute steaks, cut in serving pieces and tenderized
1 1/2 cup water
2 tablespoons onion soup mix
peeled potato halves

Roll steak pieces in flour and brown. Place in 3 qt. casserole. In skillet stir together the water & onion soup mix, loosening all the fryings. Pour over steak. Place potatoes over steak. Cover. Bake 375 1-1/2 hrs.

4 servings.

Advice from the trail:
"A two-man pup tent does not include two men or a pup."

Salt Lake Mutton Bake

Preheat oven to 475 degrees.

Take your mutton quarter, sized for the party, and put it in a turkey pan on an oak board.

Bake for 4 hours, basting every 20 minutes with a mixture of 4 eggs, 1 quart of brandy, and 2 jiggers of good bourbon.

Remove from oven & let sit for 10 minutes. **Throw away the mutton and eat the board.**

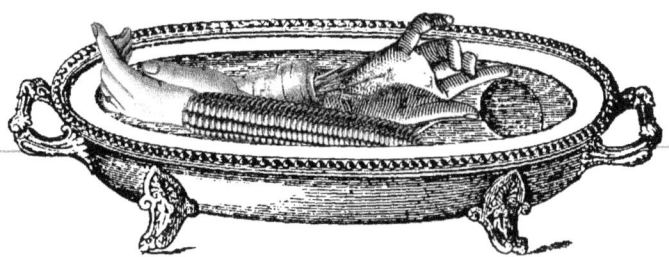

Notes

Dietary Hint: "A sweet tooth adds calcium to the diet".

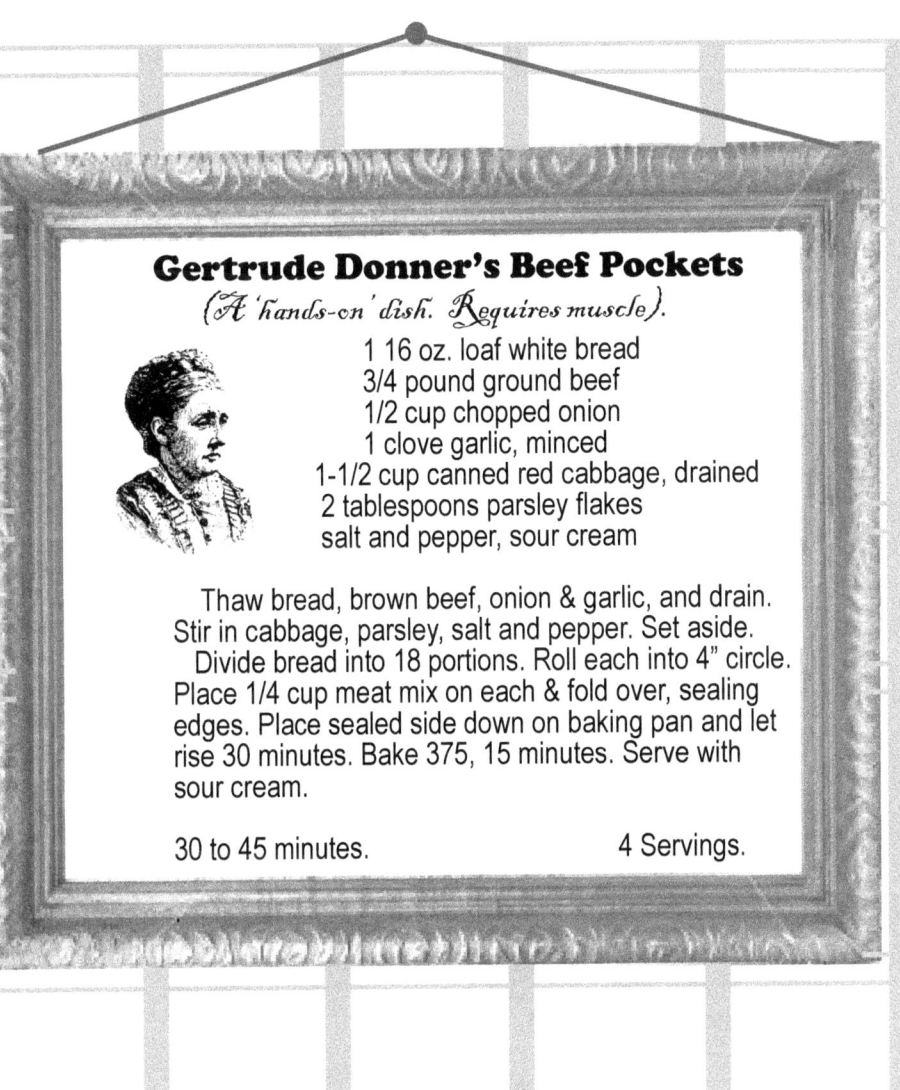

Gertrude Donner's Beef Pockets
(A 'hands-on' dish. Requires muscle).

1 16 oz. loaf white bread
3/4 pound ground beef
1/2 cup chopped onion
1 clove garlic, minced
1-1/2 cup canned red cabbage, drained
2 tablespoons parsley flakes
salt and pepper, sour cream

Thaw bread, brown beef, onion & garlic, and drain. Stir in cabbage, parsley, salt and pepper. Set aside.
Divide bread into 18 portions. Roll each into 4" circle. Place 1/4 cup meat mix on each & fold over, sealing edges. Place sealed side down on baking pan and let rise 30 minutes. Bake 375, 15 minutes. Serve with sour cream.

30 to 45 minutes.   4 Servings.

George Donner and his wife, Tamzene, started their trek with a small fortune of ten thousand dollars. Mrs. Donner sewed this nest egg into a quilt. *M-mmm, eggs...*

The Donner Party Cookbook

1846

United States *declares war on Mexico.*

Carrie Nation *is born. Famous Temperance movement activist, she was famous for destroying saloons with a hatchet.*

 **Advice from the trail:**
"Leave the oxen. Take the cannoli"

Crepes Suzette (or whomever you fancy)

(A flaming hot dish).

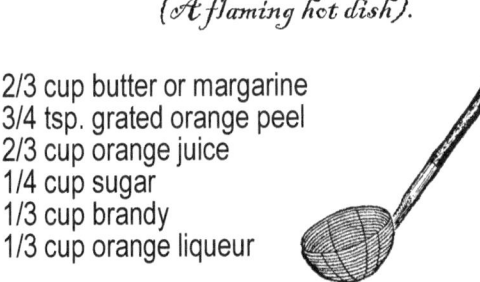

2/3 cup butter or margarine
3/4 tsp. grated orange peel
2/3 cup orange juice
1/4 cup sugar
1/3 cup brandy
1/3 cup orange liqueur

Prepare Crepes. When removing from griddle, stack so first baked side is down. Cool. keeping crepes covered to prevent them from drying out.

In 10-inch skillet, heat butter, orange peel and juice and sugar to boiling, stirring occasionally. Boil and stir one minute. Reduce heat and simmer.

In small saucepan, heat brandy and orange liqueur, but do not boil. To assemble Crepes Suzette, fold crepes into fourths; place in hot orange sauce and turn once. Arrange crepes around edge of skillet. Pour warm brandy mixture into center of skillet and ignite. Spoon flaming sauce over crepes. Place 2 crepes on each dessert plate; spoon sauce over.

6 servings.

"A surviving member of the Party got some vinegar in his ear. He was said to be suffering from pickled hearing."

The Donner Party Cookbook

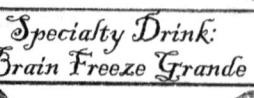

Specialty Drink:
Brain Freeze Grande

1846

PRESIDENT: James K. Polk (D)
VICE-PRESIDENT: Geo. M. Dallas (D)

Iowa *is admitted as 29th U.S. State.*

Saxophone *is patented by Adolphe Sax.*

Liberty Bell *is cracked when rung for George Washington's birthday.*

★ Pickled Organs *are found to be extra good with cheddar cheese.*

"Jimmy Crack Corn" was a popular tune, and likely sung on the trail. Aww, shucks! When it comes to a lively tune, we're all ears.

 **Tamzene's White Mountain Cake**
(Slice after slice, every layer is nice).

Bake your favorite 8 or 9-inch round layer cake. Cool.

Prepare 1 package (7.2 ounces) fluffy white frosting mix, or use store-bought tub. Fold in 1/2 teaspoon almond extract. Frost cake. Sprinkle cake with flaked coconut.

Place piece of plain paper on back of cake pan and cut out circle the size of cake. Draw Christmas tree in center of paper; cut out tree. Place circle with tree pattern on cake. Sprinkle green-tinted coconut in the tree shape, carefully following pattern. Fill base of tree with shaved chocolate. Remove circle.

Roll red gumdrops on granulated sugar until flat. With small star cutter, cut star in each gumdrop. Insert small red candles in gumdrop stars and place on branches of tree. If desired, decorate tree with silver dragees.

Advice from the trail:
"Don't squat with your spurs on."
"A closed mouth gathers no foot."

Notes

Snowy Apple Salad
(Road apples are no substitute for red delicious).

In saucepan, combine one 8 3/4-ounce can undrained crushed pineapple, 2 beaten eggs, 1/2 cup sugar, 1/4 cup water, 3 tablespoons lemon juice, and dash salt. Cook over low heat; stirring constantly, til thickened. Chill.
Stir in 2 cups diced unpared apple and 1/2 cup chopped walnuts; fold in 1 cup whipping cream, whipped. Pour into 8x8x2-inch pan. Freeze til firm. Let stand at room temperature 10 -15 minutes before serving. Cut into squares.

9 servings.

Sutter's Fort Sorbet
(The entire Party is sweet on this).

4 cups watermelon cubes, seeded
1 cup tropical fruit juice blend

Arrange watermelon cubes on jellyroll pan. Freeze until firm. Transfer to airtight container and store in freezer for up to 2 months. Place frozen watermelon in work bowl of food processor fitted with steel knife blade; process until slushy. With machine running, slowly add juice through feed tube; process until smooth. Serve immediately. Garnish with fresh mint sprigs.

4 servings.

Floss After Eating.

Overheard on the trail:
"That wasn't chicken."

Notes

Calves Foot Jelly
(No wonder the cows got mad...).

Cut the calf's feet across the 1st joint and through the hoof. Place in a large saucepan, cover with cold water, and bring quickly to a boil. When water boils, remove them & wash them thoroughly in cold water. When perfectly clean, put into a porcelain-lined sauce pan, add cold water in the proportion of 3 pts. to 2 calf's feet, and put saucepan over the fire.

When water boils, lower heat and simmer for 5 hours. Strain the liquor through a fine sieve or a coarse towel, and let it stand overnight to set. When cool, remove the fat that has risen to the top. After your queasy stomach has settled, drive to your local supermarket and buy a box of jello. It takes minutes to prepare, and comes in un-natural colors such as cobalt blue.

Those feet might look cool hanging from your rear-view mirror, though.

Overheard on the trail:
"Speaking of back home, at least our cows are sane."
"We're all in this alone."

Applesauce Relish
(A red hot delight).

1 16-ounce can applesauce
1/4 cup red cinnamon candies
1 teaspoon prepared horseradish

In saucepan, combine applesauce, candies, and horseradish. Cook and stir over medium heat till candies are dissolved. Cool; refrigerate till ready to serve.

2 cups.

30 December 1846:
Important Discovery in Surgery...

Operations have been performed upon patients in a state of insensibility from inhalation of sulphuric ether vapors.

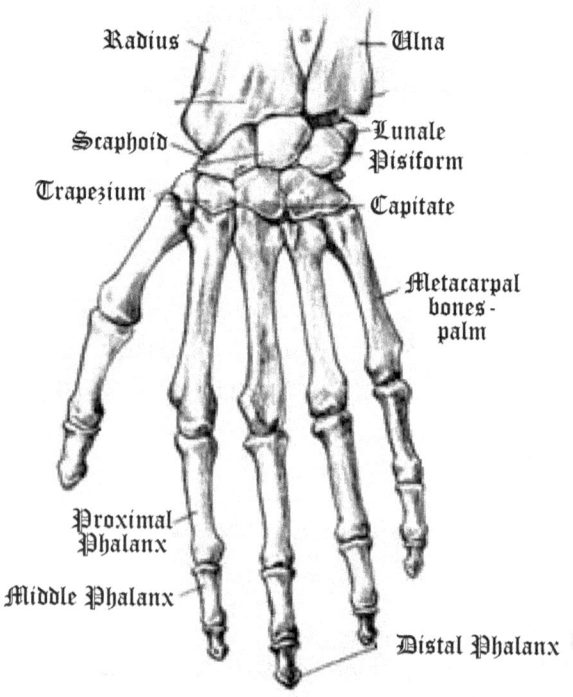

Advice from the trail:
*"When you come to the fork in the road,
better beware, me thinks.
If anyone pokes you with the tines,
just don't get stuck for drinks..."*

Helpful Hints

Put your guests at ease with a light snack-before dinner, as the grand finale to an night at the theater, or with bridge. Remember this:

"Finger foods should not be messy, especially when the guests are dressy; the rule that says what size is right is keep it down to just one bite."

How to carve a rib roast

(Invite Miley for dinner. Make it a celebrity roast).

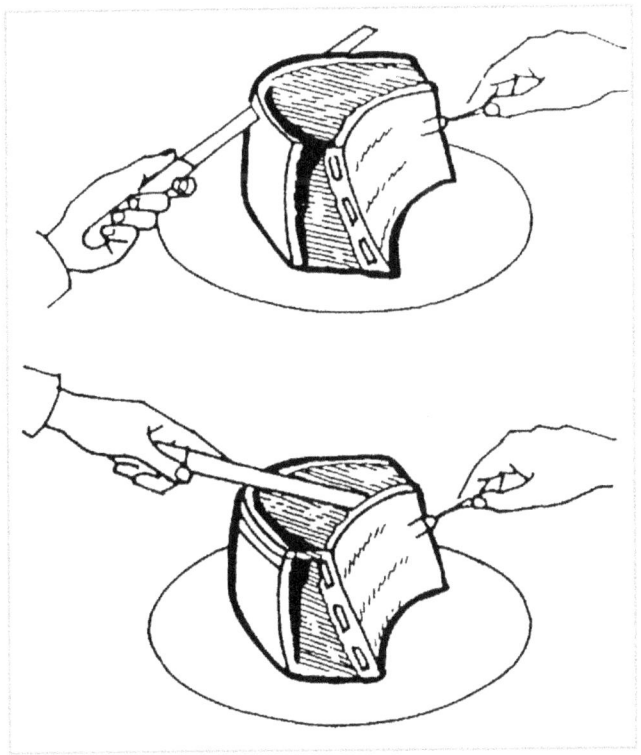

Advice from the trail:
*"To be a vegan wasn't wise:
the menu was loaded with meaty guys...
There was not a tomato,
nor a trace of potato,
but bodies were stacked to the skies."*

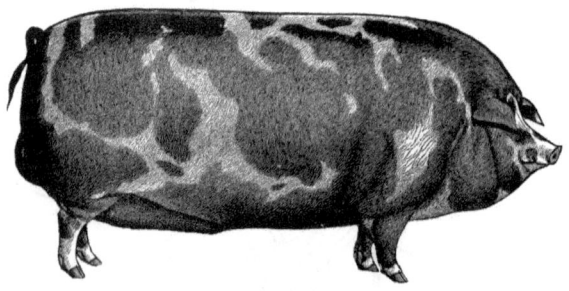

Pork: *not the only white meat.*

"Is it spoiled?"
(Even 20-foot snowdrifts can't save food forever...)

If you can tie a carrot in a knot, *throw it away.*

If the flour wiggles, *dump it.*

If a potato has more eyes than you, *plant it.*

If you open the fridge, and neighborhood dogs come running, *the meat has gone bad.*

Canned goods that are the size and shape of a basketball *should be disposed of.*

When the chicken starts pecking its way out of the shell, *the egg is past its prime.*

Raisins *should not* be harder than your teeth.

Lettuce is spoiled when it becomes *green liquid.*

Salad dressing *should not* taste like wine.

When onion dip can be taken out of the container and bounced, *it has spoiled.*

"Does this clown taste funny to you?"

Limerick from the trail:
"The dear departed had certain appeal, and hungry survivors wanted a meal. So they carved the dead, from toes to head, but no one wanted the heel."

The Donner Party Cookbook

General Housekeeping Complaint of 1846:
"Cooking is the plague of my life; my range never works well, and by the time I have prepared a meal I am fearfully hot and my appetite is gone."

 # Kitchen Hints

If you've over-salted soup or vegetables, add cut raw potatoes and discard once they have cooked and absorbed the salt.

A teaspoon each of cider vinegar and sugar added to salty soup or vegetables will also remedy the situation.

If you've over-sweetened a dish, add salt.

If you will brown the flour well before adding to the liquid when making gravy, you will avoid pale or lumpy gravy.

A pinch of baking soda added to gravy will eliminate excess grease.

Drop a lettuce leaf into a pot of homemade soup to absorb excess grease from the top.

Lettuce and celery keep longer if you store them in paper bags.

To remove the core from a head of lettuce, hit the core end once against the counter sharply. The core will loosen and pull out easily.

Cream will whip faster and better if you'll first chill the cream, bowl, and beaters well.

Cream whipped ahead of time will not separate if you add 1/4 tsp. unflavored gelatin per cup of cream.

Brown sugar won't harden if an apple slice is placed in the container.

If your brown sugar is already brick-hard, put your cheese grater to work and grate the amount you'll need.

Potatoes will bake in a hurry if boiled in salted water for 10 minutes before popping into a very hot oven.

A thin slice cut from each end of the potato will speed up baking time as well.

A Sad Chapter (& verse)...

The Donner party prepared to head west; California was their treasure chest. Plenty of land and a warmer clime; trees that grew orange, lemon and lime.

In eighteen hundred & forty-six, the passage through was tedious. Then came word of a shorter route; it sounded quite expedious.

The "Hastings cut-off" meant trouble certain; by the end of August, they were really hurtin'. Then the blizzard hit and it was bad: the worst those Sierras had ever had.

Snow piled in drifts 20 feet high. There was an ominous feeling that kin might die. While they huddled together to fight the chill, some sharpened their knives and eyed the ill.

The cattle were eaten by mid-December. Then the menu worsened, some remember. Boiled hide, twigs and bark (hardly deserving of a fork). After that, the deceased were considered. Fighting over parts left some embittered: Ezra got a thigh and Maude, the head. It had come to this: eating the dead. Tastes like chicken or maybe not, it was very tragic and never forgot.

Notes
(Preserve nature…pickle a femur).

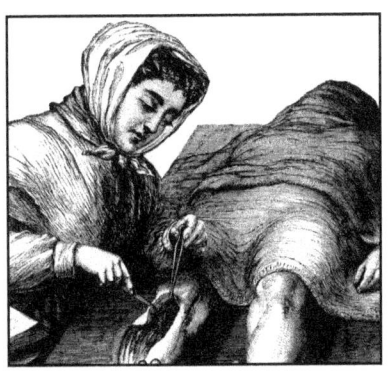

www.ingramcontent.com/pod-product-compliance
Lightning Source LLC
Chambersburg PA
CBHW071801040426
42446CB00012B/2651